# Today in the Café Trieste

## RICHARD TILLINGHAST

*Richard Tillinghast*

SALMON POETRY

Published in 1997 by
Salmon Publishing Ltd,
Cliffs of Moher, Co. Clare

© Richard Tillinghast 1997
The moral right of the author has been asserted.

A catalogue record for this book is available from the British Library.

Salmon Publishing gratefully acknowledges the
financial assistance of the Arts Council.

ISBN 1 897648 84 7 Softcover

Cover design by Estresso
Set by Siobhán Hutson
Printed by Redwood Books, Kennet Way, Trowbridge, Wiltshire

*To Thomas Lynch,*
*who netted the first salmon I ever caught*

# Acknowledgements

Acknowledgements are due to the following publications, in which a number of these poems first appeared:

*Agenda, Antaeus, The American Voice, The Boston Phoenix, The Cúirt Journal, Envoi, The Hudson Review, Lake George Arts Project Literary Review, Missouri Review, The Nation, New England Review, New Letters, The New Republic, The New Yorker, Notre Dame Review, The Other Side, The Paris Review, Partisan Review, Ploughshares, Poetry East, Sewanee Review, Southern Review, Tracks.*

'Father in October' and 'Six Mile Mountain' appeared in *Home Works: A Book of Tennessee Writers*, University of Tennessee Press, 1996. 'The Keeper' was published as a chapbook from Pym-Randall Press, Cambridge, Massachusetts, in 1968. 'Sewanee in Ruins' is a book-length poem originally published in 1981 by the University Press in Sewanee, Tennessee. The first of its five sections is reprinted here. 'Tea' originally appeared in *A Visit to the Gallery*, University of Michigan Press, 1997. Excerpts from 'Today in the Cafe Trieste' were included in *A Year in Poetry*, Crown Publishers, 1995.

The poems in Part 1 are new. The poems in Part 2 are a selection taken from three books published in the United States by Wesleyan University Press: *Sleep Watch, The Knife and Other Poems*, and *Our Flag Was Still There*.

# Contents

*Part 1*

*Part 2*

# Part I

# Six Mile Mountain

The ground held more stones than dirt.  No arrowheads,
No shaped flint-chips rose to their pick and shovel.
No one had disturbed these rocks since God and the glacier
Laid them down in anger.

They attacked the shelved-in limestone with their pick,
And flecks rained dryly down on dead oak leaves.
Dogwood misted the woods, forsythia brightened.
The stores in Six Mile were selling flowers for Easter.

Tears fell into the hole they were digging.
They sweated out last night's whiskey and grief.
In the high air's stillness that hard metallic ping
Ricocheted off tree trunks, bare and obdurate.

Finally the earth's coolness breathed up to them.
Little winged things flitted in the air above
The grave.  Thumbnail-sized black butterflies appeared.
Black-capped chickadees perched on the black limbs

And answered the sharpened cries of pick and shovel.
The day warmed.  Mare's-tails flared across the sky's
Bland cerulean.  In the air-drifts
That skimmed the ridge a hawk glided, watching.

# The World Is

The world is a man with big hands
and a mouth full of teeth.
The world is a ton of bricks, a busy signal,
your contempt for my small talk.
It's the crispy lace that hardens
around the egg you fry every morning
sunny side up.

The world is the last week of August,
the fumes that dizzy up into the heat
when you fill your tank
on the way to work late, again.
The world is 'Please take a seat over there'.
The world is 'It'll have to come out'.
The world is 'Have a nice day'.

The world is 'What is that peculiar smell?'
The world is the button that popped off,
the watch that stopped, the lump you discover and turn
    on the light.
The world is a full ashtray, the world is that grey look,
the world is the County Coroner of Shelby County.
The world is a cortege of limousines,
an old man edging the grass from around a stone.

The world is 'Belfast Says No!', the world is reliable
sources, a loud bang and shattered glass raining down
    on shoppers.
The world is a severed arm in a box of cabbages, 'And then

the second bomb went off and we didn't know which
way to run'.  The world is semtex and black balaclavas
and mouth-to-mouth resuscitation.  The world is
car alarms silenced, and a street suddenly empty.

The world is one thousand dead today in the camps.
The world is sixty thousand latrines, the world is
bulldozers pushing bodies and parts of bodies into a ditch.
The world is dysentery and cholera,
infected blood, and vomit.  The world
is mortality rates, and rape as an instrument of war.
     The world
is a 12-year-old with a Walkman, a can of Coke, and an Uzi.

# His Days

When one of his black moods bedeviled him,
When the wince of some remembered pain –
Some wrong done to him, some cruelty of his own –
Hurt him like a surge melting down
Bad wiring, what choice was left to him
But to flinch and swallow and bear it like a man?

The cottage's slates and silences became
His kingdom, its weathers his own.  He would coax
To a blaze coal and turfs each morning, and chunks
Of beech he split with his own axe.
The farmer's son or Sunday hikers would see him
Hunched at his kitchen table, away in his books.

Then obscurely one morning he'd lock his cottage door.
With a word to no one he'd be gone,
To look at an old church somewhere, or the ruin
Of a tower down a dirt track, or a stone
Incised with markings no one could decipher,
Its language crumbling by degrees in the rain.

He could navigate the old script.  And he knew why an arch
Was rounded or gothic.  Why the mermaid
Held a mirror.  Which sins the monks allowed
Themselves, and which they disavowed.
He knew the griefs of the high kings, belonged to the church
Of bitterness, had bet on the cards of pride.

But when on some grimy market town's main street
He heard a child, eyes widening in wonder,
Call out 'Daddy!', reaching for his father,
It cut him like the crack of leather.
Then, it seemed, the pain was complete.
The water was wide, and he could not swim over.

# A Visit

Mud spattered the windscreen of my rental car.
When I asked where she was buried, a memory fell
Like shade across the face of the woman who lived
In what had been the gate lodge – then a smile,
A shy welcome, and she pointed the way to the churchyard.
Then a child called her, so there was not a soul

Between me and the sand-blasted spire of the Protestant
    church.
The shape of her headstone, beveled like the gable
Of a Dutch canal-house, was, like her handwriting,
Charactered but unobtrusive.  The lichened marble
Put me in mind of the mottled green Parker with which
She used to write.  The doll's-house of a school

Stood out from the choir of the church, where Joseph in
    his coat
Of many colours was first betrayed, where Mary
'Kept all these things and pondered them in her heart'.
I peered into those depths, through cobwebbed glass
Where desks swam in the green of a river twilight.
Thumbtacked to the wall was a snapshot of her house,

Gone now, and the print of a Pre-Raphaelite
Madonna and child.  My neglect – I had let her grow old! –
Burned in my face, acknowledged now for the first time.
She was Mary in the painting, I was the child –
I could see that now – nurtured and wondered at.
Ungrateful, and leaving already, I had struggled

To step off into an air beyond her containment.
Nothing stirred in that churchyard, or gave the slightest
    impression
Her story and mine impinged on the afternoon.
I turned away, walked back to my car –
Warned off by a treeful of rooks – and drove out the gate.
How long it takes us to become who we are!

# The Emigrant

Two places only
there were:
here and America.
The four corners of the farm,
and gone-beyond-the-sea.

With a twopenny nail
he etched into the iron
shank of his spade
the word 'Destiny',
drove it with his boot smartly into the turf
and left it standing.

Abroad commenced
at the town line.
The New World blinded him
on the Navan road
and again the first time he tried to speak English
and again the first time he saw an orange.

Anaesthetized by reels and barrels of porter
and eight renditions of 'The Parting Glass',
he fell asleep to the groan of oars
and awoke to a diesel thrust
and sleet over mountainous seas.

# Legends of Lady FitzPigge-Hightits

Did God in one of his wilder flights of fancy
Ever make a woman – no matter how hard she might
Ride to hounds, no matter with how sure a hand
Skipper a yacht through gale-whipped seas, or fill
A ball gown to perfection – who could hold a candle
To Lady Hightits?

              Mornings, when I heard skirts glide
Past my schoolroom door, I'd creep out into the hall
To obsequiate and pull my forelock, leaving
The little viscounts to their hic-haec-hocs,
Shutting the door on that olfactorium
Of ink and library paste and porridge farts –

To breathe Mount FitzPigge's wider freedoms, its air
Of cut flowers and beeswax and China tea,
And Lady Foxglove's famous *potpourris*.
She'd brisk along with her plaid-kilted secretary
Beside her, jotting down notes, her English butler
Sniffing along behind, the Pekineses nipping his spats.

The things they did with their money! (most of it
From coal mines in South Wales, mind you, no matter
How many unicorns or griffins or wyverns
Quartered or pranced or buggered across their coat
Of arms).
           Fancy their building their own airfield –
Lady Windrush-Libertyscarf buzzing the lough
In her Gypsy-One Moth, Lord Stablecock buggering off

To surprise one of his actresses, or swooping
Down to Gstaad to fetch the little snotnoses
Home from skiing, in his Percival Q6
Six-seater.
                    Four chauffeurs for four cars! Not
To mention his-and-her Rollses. And the house
Packed out with guests – Vita Sackville-West
And that wet husband of hers in his stiff tweeds,
Yeats with his *pince-nez* and fluttering hands and dandruff,
Gobbling scones and ringing for endless cups of tea,
John Betjeman fogging his glasses over the Georgian
    brasswork.

Me, with my Trinity B.A. and my book
Of eclogues from Skylark Press – for afternoon tea
I got ironstone crockery and broken meats
In the servants' kitchen, the conversational arts
Of the pimply telegraph boy and under-house
Parlourmaid, wet boots, and a whiff of petrol
Off the chauffeur's tunic – except when the literary crowd
Came round, and nobody else could speak their language.

Today the Rollses have fetched up in vintage
Car collections, the house in Park Lane demolished,
An hotel put up in its place, the 12th Marquess
Ambushed on the coast road by the IRA.

But when Lady Hightits stood tiara'd at the top
Of those marble stairs, translucent as alabaster,
Receiving with the Prince of Wales on one side,
The Viceroy on the other (I lurked behind
The gladioli in a dinner jacket borrowed

From Lord Quickflask), her black-and-silver
Sequined bosom – *beaucoup du monde au balcon* –
Seemed designed by evolution and Burke's Peerage
To dazzle the world's eyes with the FitzPigge diamonds.
Every gesture of her hands flashed wristsful of sapphires.
Her dress glittered like a coat of mail.  She attacked
Like a young Crusader suited up for battle.

# Hooded Crow and Speedwell

His unblinking coal-chunk eye awake
To carrion or a young nestling fallen
His way, that self-possessed hooded fellow
Hops on the chimney-stack, ready to lurch
Out on the leathery menace of his wing-stroke.

Dream-bothered, up before the farmers,
I hunch by the fire and watch him. At lambing time
The herdsmen blast away at the crow, or throw stones.
He swoops at their shaky wool-fluff heartbeats.
Have a care for the baby. Keep the kitten indoors.

The same day, out walking, not so much to get
Anywhere as to wipe from my feet the reprimand
Of the grave I stood by in my dream, I am buoyed
Up by swells of buttercups, startled by wild orchids.
Then a downpour soaks me before I can find that

Bright-eyed blue I needed, growing
Threaded into a hedge: rained-on glances
Of speedwell – blue as the sky I wished for, purpling
To gloaming, no bigger than a baby's tooth. Why
Have I walked a mile to find it? What is it saying?

# Lexicons

Search parties, ice-axed, cramponed, dispatched
into the unfrequented high-country
   of my mental thesaurus
to pin an unthumbed word
        on the uncoined cry of
this coot I'm watching,
   who coasts among
lily pads where she has splashed down,
       churning up metaphors.

Surely her vocalized monosyllable
        is not the eponymous 'Coot!'
proposed by every bird book –
but something closer to a high-register 'Squinx!'
      as absurd officious *Fulica atra*
cruises the lake hegemonically, like a toy gunboat,
        dependencies in tow.

As we drift, as we navigate and divagate –
the coot and I –
     a pointy-eared red squirrel
scurries overhead up the *pinus radiata*
       I'm leaning against.
   It cries in alarmed contralto
    like one-inch-wide expensive grosgrain
yanked very fast, singing,
      off a milliner's cardboard spool.

# Habitat

Shine your torch between the stones here:
  a tortoiseshell butterfly, is it not? –
holed up like the rest of the self-renewing world this
      February day
    with only ourselves out for a walk.

Its wingtips serrate like the lip of a seashell –
    patterned dabs, dusky as the clove-stuck orange in the
      parlour,
like ashtray burns, brown centering to black.

I know if I take one of this butterfly's wings
    between the thumb and forefinger of each of my hands
and explicate it like a doll's fan
I can show you the big black ink-swabs
    topping each powdery wing, like single strokes of
      midnight.

But my hands are not sunshine.
    Leave the tortoiseshell,
      like a spare pair of spectacles,
folded in its crevice with eight or ten others
    in the wall of this fortified tower that half stands

    on a rise in a pasture.
Its top storeys fell, or were battered and tumbled
      downhill into a tarn,
and I don't even know where to put my hand
on the book that would tell us what baron
or cattle-thieving chieftain or shrewd abbot built it
    in which dark century, or in which campaign he lost it,

16

abandoning the position
to colonies of mosses and lichens, cow patties,
the rusted-out door of an old Morris
    propped against the wall.

A long-eared bat, *plecotus auritus*, stirs
    and propels itself out of hibernation.
Its amazing ears stand out from its head
  and it looks like a hyper-vitamined rabbit
    as it navigates its goofy flight-jags
        on wings of parchment.

Over our heads where he errs, there's a clear view –
    no ceiling left after five hundred years –
to a huge untidy bundle of kindling
    lodged above a fireplace big enough
        to roast two sheep in.
A raven on nest creaks her settled wings and croaks
    down at us.

    The male deploys in a lancet window,
a choker of sable ruffed about his neck.
    His beak makes him feudal, *sub rosa*, a henchman –
outwardly a study in resignation,
        but versed in the code of *duello*.

Ravens lay their eggs in February –
                think of the caution of it.
No flowers bloom yet, of any kind, to line
    their unassailable nest. Certainly not!

# Currency

No bed for me in this city tonight, no key
in my pocket for anyone's door.
No cure for the rain
that revives the dusty quayside sycamores
and wears away the faces
on statues of the famous dead.

Decades gone, I'd amble these quays,
jingling the harps and salmons in my pockets,
my sense of pure form freshened
by vertical parallels of 18th-century brick
that stripe the currents of rippled dull jade
careering down to the Irish Sea
between banked, peeling trunks
of river-drinking trees.

I must have blinked, though,
because now two girdered cranes,
one immemorial blue, one summer-camp green,
wrecking the lovely city brick by brick,
wheel in a cluttered sky
as weepy as the sad watercolours
my dead aunt used to paint.

The key changes, clouds modulate, sunshine
recurs. My footsteps
evanesce from the cobblestones.

# Westbound

First a startle of fragrances
to remind me where I am:
turf smoke blown through drizzle,
oystery brine-tang over Quay Street.

An umbrella-raking gale.
Then mind-blowing blue above the town for a nanosecond
    until my airport-bound rented windscreen
        spatters with the weather's wet
      splash of anticipation and
by an astral lope I'm back in a place with trees where

I picture you holding open a Victorian door shyly –
    then an almost imperceptible bouquet
        of lavender and myrrh
      from between your thighs.

Two virtues of a Catholic girlhood:
the name Mary, and secrets in the dark.

 This far away I can touch the hard nubby stars
of chrysanthemums that I put in the ground,
      watered and husbanded. They bud up now.

            Petit Sirah
and, as a present for you, notecards
    with Kilkenny rooks
        settling among smoky chimney-stacks and
    copper beeches.

But how can I write on flat paper
this impulse that arcs between us, inarticulately,
        as I fly?

# Am I Like a Tree

planted by the water
in this congregation, in my father's glen plaid jacket?
What are these other
well-dressed communicants doing here?

My camel would balk at any attempt
to drive him through the eye of a needle.
What good would it do
to abandon my father and my mother,
now both gone anyway,
and give my worldly goods to be sold?

Yet I think I know what it means
to take up my cross daily.

What am I to make of this advice
to seek first the kingdom of Heaven?
The paths of righteousness
are brambled over, are they not?
Rocky, and the footing is bad.

Yet even I have sat down among stones
rough-hewn into blocks two cubits on a side,
and counted my money out in my hands
to see if I could pay to have my tower built.

Asters, I think it is,
on the altar. Someone has laundered and starched the cloth
and now it reflects whitely up onto the silver chalice
as I would expect it to do
at a luncheon in Heaven.

Though I may join my voice with angels and archangels
and all the company of Heaven, evermore praising
Thee and singing this hymn to proclaim the glory
of Thy holy name;
and though I may even be allowed sometimes
to drink the cup of salvation
and eat the bread of Heaven,
I could never really cut it
as a disciple.

Step sure-footedly.
Be a tree with roots.
Have money in your hand.
Kneel.  Rejoice.

We all know one fine morning
we will be called on
in one breath
to renounce all that we have.

# Father in October

*for Brownie and Kate*

When the smell of freshly sharpened pencils had lost
Its power to intoxicate, when our first
Infatuation with September had slackened –
With its satchels and homework and new teacher;
When the leaves of the late-blooming chrysanthemums
In our frost-finished back garden had blackened,
One morning my mother would retrieve our winter
Hats and scarves, our gloves and heavy raingear.
My father would go up attic, bring down the storms
And snug them in, between ourselves and the weather.

One hundred years of our family had lived
Beneath that house's airy ceilings, had sat
By a grate where coal sputtered and glowed in the glass
Cases where my grandfather's books were shelved –
Shakespeare, the Brontës, Dickens, Sir Walter Scott.
And the house told stories, of interest only to us:
The well, sealed after Uncle John drowned a cat.
The deep-cut initials my older brother carved
Above the stairs. The bed my mother was born in.
Every dip in the floorboards spoke, every curious stain

Remembered. To marry my mother, my father found
In 1932, was to husband her house.
Its *fin de siècle* wiring was a fireman's nightmare;
What was airy in June was draughty in December.
'Manage', 'Simplify', his granite New England

Eyes said.  Those Willifords must have seemed another
Species altogether – with their Southernness,
Their leaky roof, their Eastlake furniture.
There was hardly a marble-topped table that didn't wobble,
Or a chair that couldn't have used some glue or a nail.

Saturdays he'd be up by six.  First
A shave, and with his shaving brush he'd soap
Clean the lenses of his gold-rimmed glasses.
Then he'd collect himself over coffee and make a list,
Numbered and neat, of his day's projects in the shop
He had built out back under the hickory trees.
A nimbus of sawdust surrounding his concentration,
He'd turn a chair-leg on his lathe, cut out
A bracket or brace with his jigsaw, then fashion
A toy pistol for me, or a paddle-wheel boat.

Daddy's real work was engineering.  His own
Dreams and epiphanies came to him, I imagine,
In the language of his calling – straightedged and clear
As a blueprint, verifiable by time and motion
Studies.  His few inventions that made a profit,
The many he drew in his mind but had to give
Up on, lived a life pristine and platonic –
Not subject to half-measures or the change of season,
Not battered by weather or in need of repair
Like the mortal house I judged him master of.

# Starfuckers

'Isn't it time I slipped my leash?'
    she thought.        For him, what was it?
A quickening.  A corner he hadn't turned.

Their hands, their eyes, their mouths,
        each discreet designer bruise,
pronounced each other's body canonical.

While at the same time knowing
    love is the sublimest form of stupidity,
they looked into each other's eyes
as if refining the expression
        on a self-portrait.

The way she formed her letters made his breath catch.
The postman was a chubby little cupid.

    They were both
        starfuckers.

'Your lower lip drives me wild',
she said in a trattoria.

# Osmanli

The parade-ground elegance of her conjugations
thickened my tongue.
Her declensions were a *corps de ballet*.

Bearing in our thorn-cut hands
roses to place on the grave of an infant
we ascended, foot-wobbly from hours in her bed,
flights of stairs jungled in jasmine,
shattered in the War of Independence –
through an acre of yew trees, marble turbans snapped off
    their shafts,
sculpted Aeolian harps, conquered Paschal lambs.

Apexing, next morning, the iron filigree bridge
between her Europe and her Asia
I would sigh upward into the Iznik of a sky
four provinces Balkan,
six districts Mediterranean.

When my lips formed the possessive couplet –
her most characteristic construction –
my nostrils widened to a suggestion
part river-drinking plane trees, part sea-tang, part
    sunburned thyme.

Pronouncing her – even as poorly as I did –
sheathed me in the hauteur of vanished empire.

How could I return then
to the diphthongs and parataxis of my homeland?

# Tea

Erase a statue of Buddha, eyes lidded on nonexistence.
Erase topiary.
Take away red paint and gilding if you can.

This is a place to sit for a while,
the mats fresh,
smell of rain in rushes.

A crane glides without moving its wings
over the stream's length.
Peonies bloom in silk.

Is the stream a part of nature, or has it been
altered by the sages?
A shower blows up among cypresses up trail.

The tea master is away.
Otherwise how should I be here?

Over foothills scrolling,
mist brightens and evanesces.
Families of monkeys move over the ridge above,
through jungle, mist frozen on their muzzles.

Brown smoke from cooking fires
finds a path up here
from where the nomads camp.
God knows what they are burning.

Then the clear green tea:
green like water at the bottom of the ocean,
but hot as a bowl of soup.

Behind us, the trek over the mountains,
hand-drawn maps, bad knees and brambles.

Who knows what thundery warlord or dakini
caused the wind to blow the clouds
from one side of the mountain to the other?

Where the trail switchbacks above us,
two immortals play at chess.

# Opera on Jukebox

*Café Trieste, San Francisco*

'*Un Bel Di Vedremo*' finishes
and then '*Una Furtiva Lacrima*'
swallow-tails through the café
recasting tobacco walls as tiers of boxes
like the bosoms of the convent school's senior class
lined up in presentation mode for the big evening out.
The soprano's semi-quavers dagger
Neapolitan bedchamber velvets,
and the blood of cousins flows.

This the music must accomplish
to the accompaniment of two massive exhaust fans
stirring a power of roasted coffee beans.
Out high transom windows one glimpses two flags –
ours, and the Italian tricolour's vertical stripes:
white like the clouds against which it appears,
green like malice, red like the heart
as it empties and fills.

# The Red Cottage

What we've called the red cottage
Since way back before we were follicly challenged
Is brown now.  Burned down and rebuilt.
I can trudge upriver and fish at 'the tractor seats'
But they were removed from the bank
When my boys were in Cub Scouts.

Blink, and I see the eerie burnishment
Like a sunset occluded, at midday:
The forest fire as it approached,
Burning the red cottage to the ground
While the flames leapt over the top of Martin's three
Cottages, where we stay.
Our years there were not burned.

On Downriver Road the Mom & Pop
Is owned by a new mom & pop.
Along the banks, animal and fishermen's
Paths run, a community of destinations.
Might they not be the city plan of Paris
Four thousand years ago?  Or the nascent grid of a
     metropolis
Next millennium, Dark Age streets hoof- and foot-beaten
     into the marsh,
Furtive little doglegs through tag alders and larch.

The Hendrickson hatch comes on in May, or else
It does not.  Or else it does
And you are not in the river then,
Taking a nap or writing poetry or hunting morels.

We mix the same martini still, and slow-cook the meat of
    the pig.
Or else it rains, and only undeterred diehards
Are out in a slicker, casting a green
Feather wrapped with sparkles,
Flashing it over gravelly shallows.

Or you read obscure back numbers of *Field and Stream*
Or craft, on a fly-tying vise,
Hendricksons, each trig as a sailboat,
Wings transparent as the lights of a Japanese teahouse,
White-and-brown hair of something, tufted–
Then the spinner, spent wings finished, sprawled out
Dead on the river that pours and pours downstream.

# Wireless

Anchorite of insomnia,
3 AM exile thumbing a skyful
Of shortwave radio
Static, through unidentifiable
Squiggles and blurted Morse, I nudge the dial
Millimetre by millimetre
Across a spatter

Of languages – three different Englishes –
Goldberg variations, a hemisphere's
Weather and news flashes,
While a gale off the North Atlantic tears
At my island's landward moorings, and roars
Through every frequency
In the crackling sky.

Only a thread keeps me from slipping
Anchor, from floating like an imaginary
Iceberg out to sea, sleeping
Toward Greenland, or adrift entirely–
Unmoored beyond these signals, this rosary
Of stations.  A finger's touch
Keeps me attached.

# The Button

That button dangled:
threadwork of a spider
who had flunked her Home Ec. course.
My jacket, already a size too loose,
lagged off one shoulder
as if blown by an August wind.

Needle and thread I needed, sharpness
and extension, penetration and follow-through.
First bought a black pig-snout of a spool.
Then Sarah looked in the kitchen and found
in the third drawer down, her mother's needle –
unbending, a fairy pikestaff.

Outdoors, while swallows and house martins swooped
near enough to tell them apart –
treble twitter of the swallow from the dull 'stirrup'
of the martin – I poked, slow-fingered seamster,
the snub needle nose through corduroy
and secured that errant discus of bone.

Then put the jacket on again,
drew together the two halves of my person,
fastened that essential button,
and walked off into what awaited.

# Part 2

# The Creation of the Animals

We were angels before the sky lost us
When it happened I touched myself
My hands were new     were not hands
We spoke sounds that no one understood
that were no longer words

He would come and watch our mouths learning the food
He gave us     in love with his own brilliance
Using his power had left him innocent
and he thought he had made us from nothing
not missing us     not knowing he had blundered
and we had fallen from the sky like tiles from a mosaic
never dreaming his strength
had struck out beyond his will

Later on     when he saw that things had gone wrong
beyond his power to restore them
it rested him to look at us
And I found I could love him in his weakness
as I never could before
The beauty left his face     and his eyes began to cloud
with the grief that killed him

I ran on the grass     made paths through the woods
felt the rain in my fur
Remembering the golden cities no longer moves me
I begin to forget     I flew once     and knew the order
of a beauty
I no longer have the mind for.

# The Keeper

Our animals are sleeping.
The eyes of the dog move    dreaming    his paws
shuffle feebly
about his nose,
And the cat's long sleeping noise
so low as not to be heard, and treble.

I drift in the chair    drowsy
while the others are sleeping,
a family
drawn up in their beds and cozy
their future devolving on me
as a kindness – the one who answers, the keeper.

Rain on the pavement and roofs of sheds.
One thinks of bluegills slurping gnats
and little frogs among the lily pads.
Time lapses    impossible to picture
the dial of a clock existing anywhere
except perhaps

vastly
the numerals curiously wrought    pale green
against the stars    The hands glide into vision
now here    now there    and scarcely
give the appearance of motion
describing an imaginary plane.

I stare
no farther than my glasses    The mirrored eye
looks through    lidless    having no lash of hair
Behind the glassy sky
it never closes    or opens,    and keeps
us.    It neither slumbers nor sleeps.

# Passage

1.


The essence of gasoline is in the streets.
Plastic china is on sale, and cars full of chihuahuas.
In the house with telephones,
no one can see beyond the windows
where taxis cruise,
their headlights mooning on our ceiling
like aquarium lights.


2.


Behind these things        beneath the voices at a fire
is an engine cutting down        all vibration
the pistons lapsing in their cylinders.
Inside all radiators –        the dripping and knocking –
ignoring the stone dome of resonance
where leaded metal sloshes deeply,
must be such a passage as this:
green, inarticulate, subterranean –
seals ducking in and out the waters,
brighteyed fish breathing upward.

Quieter than the paths of a formal garden,
quieter than a map of New Hampshire,
is this falling off.
We wonder about nothing that does not smooth our eyes.
Here is a single tulip alone, and red.

Impenetrable darkness –
when you pass your hand before your eyes
there is not even the illusion of sight.
The extinguished lamps are left behind –
one moves by touch
through the narrow sandstone tunnels.
When our cat was gone,
I heard her drowned voice everywhere
crying down the gently sloshing paths of stone.


3.


Miles above is the real
sea        and a happiness we never know –
the happiness of ants on white paper,
the mind pliant
like blank film lying in solution.

Green water        blue water
the bubbles surfacing like marble.
Patterns like smoke rising in a cobalt sky.
Yet they are flat, and sway gently for miles around the ship –
a brightness coming off the air.

At night,
in the ocean night
when ever so briefly
we break the water –
    down paths of bluish fire
    through clouds of invisible seaweed,
the terrible phosphorous rising for the moon.

# Less Than Yesterday, More Than Tomorrow

Rising from sickness
my bones thin, bending, tender to the touch,
a lightness in the inner ear

Things seem to rush at me.
I huddle away from them, my mother driving –
the street is shocking to the wheels.

They are solicitous, the potted plants
lean towards me, older.
I can see what they were thinking,

They thought ...
The smiling nurses smiled and looked in all directions
when I was shaved, a necktie, erect on my feet.

Now for a while I possess this room –
the sofa and the fire are mine, lighting the fire
is totally my province.

The floor floats, at sea.
In the window glass lake water, dry leaves floating.
The globe is out of date.

Less and less I feel I am falling forward.
My mother is less patient,
my father will send me to Florida.

For them I am closing the door to the place
where the dead children are stored,
where the pets have gone to Heaven.

# In the Country You Breathe Right

and sleep
in a single breath
the length of the darkness.

Things are
as you remember them –
a calf drinking milk that sloshes through a sieve
a cat running down a well
ferns growing through a roof.
You can hear a leaf
scrape
down the road forty feet.

Everything is wood smoke
and the smell of planked fish.
The fire logs hiss
into the river.

Our shoes are muddy
from when we fed the horses –
wifely, uxorious
they steamed in the March air
as they turned away toward the forest.

My hands are so cold
I hope you can read this.


*(for Luke Myers)*

# Return

1.


Sunburst cabbage in grey light
        summer squash bright as lemons
red tomatoes splitting their skins
     five kinds of chilies burning in cool darkness,
    sunflower lion's-heads
        in the blue Chevy pickup.

Hands shaking from the cold
     turn on the headlights; he starts
      down the drive –

A dust you can't see
     settles over the garden and empty cabin

       silent, unnoticed
       like snow after midnight –

Power shut off in the pumphouse
     tools suspended over light-blue silhouettes
     he has painted for each of them.

Dark trees stand
     and watch his old truck
      bump down the hill.

Behind him:    star-fall he's not sure he saw,
    bone-chill flute
      certainty of dawn.

He feels the pecans, the wild hazelnuts
                the small but hard and juicy apples
        in the oversized pockets of his coat,
                the cloth worn soft as rabbit-fur.


White dairy-fences border his way,
                AM radio farm news,
        placidness of black-nosed sheep in ground-fog,
                mist rising over bluegrass.


He drives by Tomales Bay.
        The old fisherman scowls at the low sky and waves,
                squinting to keep out the
        wreathing, first-cigarette smoke.


        Squirrels
        flash down tree-trunks
when they see him coming –
        Farmers turn on their lights.


Seeds sprout in the upholstery.
                Tendrils and runners leap out
        from under his dashboard –


He sails past the whitewashed stumps
                from the 1906 earthquake,
past the old hotel at Olema,
        stops for a whizz at Tocaloma,
        because of the name.

Sycamore leaves are falling,
I feel them rustling
around his shoulders
and wreathing his hair.

The shepherd with eyes like his
wakes up in a field.
The farmer goes out to milk,
his cold hands pink on the pink freckled udders.

The fisherman he could almost be
lets down nets into dark water

and brings up the trout-coloured dawn.


2.


For a few miles on the freeway we
float in the same skin,
he and I.
But the sun rises in my
rearview mirror.
I'm myself now.
I cross the bridge and pay my toll.

The city draws me like a magnet –
first the oil refineries,
the mudflats and racetrack by the Bay,
the one-story houses,
then a vision of you waking up:
cheeks reddening, your black hair long,

your eyes that remind me of Russia,
                    where I've never been –
        as you look out at
                silvery rain on the fuchsias.


I find your house by feel.
    How many years are gone?
Your name is gone from the mailbox.
The tropical birds and palm trees and Hawaiian sunset
    you painted with a small brush
are peeling off the beveled glass door.


Forever must be over.
I get into the truck with the good things
        somebody has left here,
                and drive off into the rain –
my left hand asking my right
                a question I could never answer.

# The Knife

*for David Tillinghast*


What was it I wonder?
  in my favourite weather    in the driving rain
    that drew me like a living hand
What was it
  like a living hand
that spun me off the freeway
    and stopped me
  on a sidestreet in California
with the rain pelting slick leaves down my windshield


to see the words of my brother's poem
    afloat on the bright air,
  and the knife I almost lost
    falling end over end through twenty years
      to the depths of Spring River –


the knife I had used to cut a fish open,
      caught in time
  the instant where it falls
      through a green flame of living water.


My one brother,
      who saw more in the river than water
  who understood what the fathers knew,
      dove from the Old Town canoe
  plunged and found his place
      in the unstoppable live water

seeing with opened eyes
    the green glow on the rocks
        and the willows running underwater –
    like leaves over clear glass in the rain –


While the long-jawed, predatory fish
  the alligator gar
watched out of prehistory
  schooled in the water like shadows
    unmoved in the current,
  watched unwondering.


    The cold raw-boned, white-skinned boy
  curls off his dive in deep water
    and sees on the slab-rock
filling more space than the space it fills:


    the lost thing     *the knife*
  current swift all around it


and fishblood denser than our blood
  still stuck to the pike-jaw knifeblade
which carries a shape like the strife of brothers
        – old as blood –
    the staghorn handle smooth as time.


    Now I call to him
        and now I see
  David burst into the upper air
gasping as he brings to the surface our grandfather's knife
    shaped now, for as long as these words last,
        like all things saved from time.

I see in its steel
the worn gold on my father's hand
the light in those trees
the look on my son's face     a moment old

like the river     old like rain
older than anything that dies can be.

# The Thief

The thief came down
  through the avenue of dreams.
He took my battered gold,
  my blood-hued jewels from before
    the Revolution –
things I could never get back –

And the vine-covered jungle temple
  that the blind lady told me about:
my sword in one hand,
  in one hand the steaming, bloody virgin heart
      still beating ...

In the days after,
  on the dusty backroads and crossroads
      in the palms of my hands,
the salt-sweat stars glistened
        at midday;
I felt the speckled wisdom
of East Anglian saints and elders,
  the Word in the shadow of a doorway,
the world swaying in a pail of well-water.

The bees sang in the pines,
  loud in the sunlit open places.

I wake in a cold halo of sweat.
But wasn't I awake already? –
trembling and glancing around in fright
  like deer in the canyon
which also are gone,
crashing off gazelle-like into the trees.

Glass shattered out all around me,
    glass stuck to my fingers,
I'm wiping my eyes –

It's really gone!
I'm sitting up in bed.

Through the huge smashed pane,
    moon over ocean pasture,
Pacific roaring over me.

I'm grinning and bowing like Old Fezziwig
and shaking the hands of flies and bees
  as they pick through the remnants.

Many things that were mine
        are gone.
In my sleep the cat comes purring.
His happiness is, he says,
        as important as mine.
And in sleep comes the thief

leaving me in the care of
the little blind lady in the sunset
and the Chinese postmaster
and the man who says
  'Stay afterward.
I have an introduction for you
that will make everything clear.'

# Aspens and a Photograph

Winding down from fourteen thousand feet
through melting slush and Rocky Mountain tundra,

suddenly: white flesh of new aspens –
              and a photograph I still see
        from an attic in Trinidad,
              Colorado.

Around bends in the road,
              between the blue distances of sky,
              coveys of aspen.
Their leaves flutter all at once in the wind:
              small wing-beats in fear.

Green aspens – tall, root-tough,
  wind-graced and swayed in the blustery weather.
Right up against granite,
    saplings springing up through snow.

The photograph:
two girls' faces from 1881
in a house that raised six generations on silver –
their black gowns, aprons, their Chinese embroidery –
    only daughters
              smiling thinly into the black camera,
holding in their laps, as a kind of joke,
      long-barrelled pistols.

# Hearing of the End of the War

*1.*

Clouds dissolve into blueness.
    The Rockies float like clouds,
white ridge over blue,
    in the shimmery blue heat.

The moon floats there still
    like some round marble relic,
its classic face rubbed away by time.

A stranger arrives, all the way from Denver.
       We feed him.
He tells us that the war is over.

For years I have stopped to wonder
    what it would feel like now.
And now I only hear the slight noise
      the moment makes,
    like ice cracking,
as it flows behind me into the past.

2.

I go to the well
    and draw up a bottle of homemade beer.
The coldness from thirty feet down
      beads out wet on the brown bottle.

Breathing dusty pine fragrance,
　　　I pop open the beer, and drink
till my skull aches from the coldness.

Rubbed white dust is on plum skins
　　　as they ripen,
　　　　　green wild blueberries
　　growing from the rocks.

Wind blows in off the peaks,
　　　high in the dust-flecked sun-shafts
　　that light up the dark trees.
Rustlings and murmured syllables from other days
　　　pass through and linger
　　　and leave their ponies
　to roam among the trees and graze the coarse grass
　　　off the forest floor.

Treetop breezes, and voices
　　　returning home
　from a fight somebody lost in these mountains
　　　a hundred and ten years ago –

　A horse cries out,
　　　loose in the woods,
　　　　　running and free.
His unshod hooves thud
　　　on the hard-packed dirt.

And then each sound drops away
　– like a dream you can't even remember –

　deep behind the leaves of the forest.

*3.*

From bark-covered rafters
  white sheets hang squarely down,
dividing the still afternoon into rooms
    where we sleep, or read,
    or play a slow game of hearts.

Everyone is unbuttoned and at their ease.

  The baby's clear syllables
    rise into space:
  milky    like the half-moons
    on his tiny fingernails,

    finer than fine paper.

A new life breathes in the world –
    fragile, radiant,
  unused to the ways of men.

From halfway down the valley
    bamboo flute notes rise    float
      flutter
        and shatter
    against the Great Divide.

# Shooting Ducks in South Louisiana

*for David Tillinghast*

The cold moon led us coldly
 – three men in a motorboat –
down foggy canals before dawn
        past cut sugarcane in December.

        Mud-banks came alive by flashlight.
Black cottonmouth moccasins
 – the length of a man in the bayou –
slid into black water, head high,
  cocky as you might feel
stepping out on Canal Street
 going for coffee at 4 A.M.
        at the *Café du Monde*.

An Indian trapper called to us
 from his motorized pirogue,
        Cajun French on his radio –
taking muskrat, swamp rat, weasel,
        'anything with fur'.

Marsh life waking in the dark:
gurgling, sneaking, murdering, whooping –
  a muskrat breast-stroking through weeds toward food,
    his sleek coat parted smooth by black satin water –
frogs bellowing, bulbous waterlilies adrift
    cypresses digging their roots into water-borne ooze
dark juices collapsing cell-walls,
    oil rigs flaring thinly at daybreak.

Light dawned in our hunting-nerves.
We called to the ducks in their language.
They circled, set wing, glided into range.
    Our eyes saw keener.
Our blood leaped.  We stood up and fired –
    and we didn't miss many that day,
        piling the boat between us with mallards.


The whole town of Cutoff ate ducks that Sunday.
    I sat in the boat,
        bloody swamp-juice sloshing my boots,
          ears dulled by the sound of my gun, –
and looked at a drake I had killed:
    sleek neck hanging limp,
        green head bloodied,
    raucous energy stopped.
I plucked a purple feather from his dead wing,
and wore the life of that bird in my hat.

# Lost Cove & The Rose of San Antone

Evening comes on. I put on a clean white shirt
and feel how well it fits me. I pour bourbon,
with spring water from a plastic jug,
and look out sliding glass doors
at green suburban hills blurred with smog.
Two watches lie on the table before me:
one set for now, one telling time in 1938,
their glass faces reflecting the round California sky.

The man I see through the eye of the second watch
sits in a silence too deep for my nerves
and stares out at twilight
fading on trunks of pine and oak.
The black Model-A car rusts into the stream
that runs past his cabin in Lost Cove, Tennessee.
He reaches for the whiskey on the table,
and his sleeve clears a path through pine-needles and dust.

The coal that tumbles out of his hillside
soils the air and brick houses in Nashville.
Words burn in the rain there
from the power of water that runs past his door.
He looks at his watch and turns on the radio.
The music reaches him, all the way from Nashville.
He holds his glass of whiskey up to the light
that is almost gone. Its colour suits his thoughts.

The fiddles and autoharp fill up the dark room
and push out through paint-blackened screens
into black oaks that press against the house.
His face hurts me. It doesn't look right.
He goes against the grain
of whiskey he has made himself, and rides
the wire-song of a steel guitar through small towns,
through the bug-crowded air of farm-crossings late at night.

The disembodied, high guitar line swims in his nerves
like a salmon up a flint-rock stream,
falls like a hawk on blood.
The whiskey burns and soothes.
His tongue starts to move to the words of the song:
trains and big woods and bottomless rivers,
hard drinking, broken hearts, and death.
His blood knows whose song this is.

He's never swum in no bottomless river,
or rode that night train to Memphis,
or sat and stared at those thirteen unlucky bars.
But he sees the moon rise, with the Rose of San Antone
tattooed on it in blood.
A waitress in Denver glides toward him with drinks on
    a tray.
He stumbles, drunk, through strange woods by an airport
and walks out in San Francisco with a gun in his pocket ...

The moon sets, over hills cold and unfamiliar.
I shut off the radio, and hear the sea-roar of the freeway.
Who is this man I have dreamed up?
I cork the bottle, and get up and lock the door.

# Things Past

Ten years into memory, a house
  in the bright fluid
time – dark grain of walnut, dark
women's bodies
    in paintings by sisters.

1632 Walnut Street:
  the solid multiples of eight
    like a vintage Oldsmobile,
the curves of the numbers,
  the porch, the porch-roof lighted,
shaped a little by memory –
  lit up like a jukebox,
like an oldfashioned sunset.

Wood-doves murmur in the eaves
    as we wake.
Leaf-shadows     sun-circles
  glide over the white ceiling
    from outside our lives.

On the white terrace
  Ruthie brushes out her thick hair
    straight and blonde.
Between storms: January sunlight
  rare cloud-rainbows
    the air like a telescope
trained on the rain-wet Berkeley hills.

Mexican smoke curls
over the drifting walnut grain.
Sisters, Maurya and Tamara, –
  your voices, your names!

I drive by the house in the rain
    tonight
and see myself at the kitchen table.
As I write,
  my notebook rests on an open cookbook.
My beard curls
  in the steamy air
of Christmas turkey soup they are cooking.

Janis Joplin still sings    *Love
      is like a ball and chain!*
The guitar solo
    cuts through the years
like a pulsating river of acid.

They're drinking coffee together,
    and talking about the weather
  that squally, blowsy Berkeley night.
I can hardly see myself
  for the steam gathering on the glass.

## Summer Rain

Summer rain, and the voices of children
    from another room.
Old friends from summers past,
we drink old whiskey and talk about ghosts.
The rain ebbs, rattles the summer cottage roof,
  soaks the perished leaves in wooden gutters,
then gusts and
    drowns our fond talk.
It's really coming down, we chatter,
  as though rain sometimes rose.
The power fails.
We sit under darkness, under the heavy storm.
Our children – frightened, laughing –
  run in to be beside us.

The weak lights surge on.
We see each other's children newly.
How they've grown!    we prose
with conventional smiles, acceptingly commonplace,
  as they go back to playing.
Yet growing is what a child does.

And ourselves?
You haven't changed a bit,
  we not exactly lie,
meaning the shock is not so great
    as we'd expected.
It's the tired look around the eyes,
the flesh a little loose on the jaw ...

Your oldest daughter's a senior at Yale.
We're like our grandparents and our parents now,
    shocked by the present:

A buggy without a horse to pull it?
              A man on the moon?
          Girls at Yale?
We say goodnight. I can hardly lift
    my young son anymore
as I carry him to the car asleep.

The rain comes down, comes down, comes down.
One would think it would wear the earth away.
You told us about a skeleton
    you awoke seeing –
the dawn light on the bone.
It wakes me this morning early.
But I'm sure it wasn't a ghost, you said
    in your sensible way,
It was just my terrible fear of death.

Rain roars on the broad oak leaves
  and wears away the limestone.
I smell the mildewed bindings
  of books I bought as a student.
How shabby, how pathetic they look now
  as they stand there on their shelves unread!
Children are all that matters, you said
  last night, and I agreed.
The children's play-song – repetitive, inane –
  keeps sounding in my head.
I get up – last night's spirits alive
  this morning in my blood –
and write these perishing words down
in the voice of summer rain.

# Sovereigns

*After Rilke*

The sovereigns of the world are old,
and die without heirs.
Their pale sons die behind guarded doors.
Their daughters yield weak crowns to violence;
they break in the rough hands of the people.
The haughty, beefcattle faces bleed
  into eagles and hammers.

New money, new metal, new rulers –
the old glitter just beyond reach:
rows of decorations on white dress uniforms.
They reincarnate as gears
to turn the machine of the world.

But luck is beyond possessing.

The metal is wild, and homesick.
Each day is one day less
until it disappears
from the mints and factories
that show it so poor a life.
From bank-vaults, from inside clocks,
in dreams it runs again
through slow arteries inside mountains.
The heart pauses,
and pumps it back to the source.

# Today in the Café Trieste

*Behind the red lacquered gates,*
*wine is left to sour, meat to rot.*
*Outside these gates*
*lie the bones of the frozen and starved.*
*The flourishing and the withered*
*are just a foot apart.*
*The thought of it is an open wound.*

— Tu Fu, 8th century

*The Mountain Goddess, if she is still there,*
*will see the world all changed.*

— Mao Tse-tung, 1956

Today in the Café Trieste,
   in San Francisco, I watch through high rippled windows
     flawed and old
the blue sky that reveals
     and resembles nothing.


A face in the mirror:
  someone else's for an instant
    as I order coffee.
A smile-line cuts the flesh on the left side
   like a scar
  in an otherwise balanced face,
as though everything I've smiled at,
     or accepted with irony,
pulled me toward one side of the universe.
My face returns my stare blankly.

I slip back into it.
The light slips off my lenses,
   the marine light of the hot afternoon,
    a little too bright for the wine
  I drank last night.

Mrs. Giotta says something in Italian:
*La vita*, life –
  or the world, *il mondo*,
  I think she is saying –
  is a solid, well-made glass.
This Italian lady sets a warm glass
    of something
    in front you,
and you know the world is in order.
When order goes,
glass is the first thing to break.

Mindlessly I watch
  the North Italian daughter-in-law
    open the dishwashing machine
and roll out a tray
  on one-inch plastic wheels –
a tray of dishes like a story
    about the future of the world,
like Buenos Aires' walled-off gardens
    seen from a private plane.
In the upturned tops of green stemware –
  jade lakes, limpid
    half-moons
  of hot water, cooling,
 redolent of jungle spring,
  clean steam rising in the café.

The daughter-in-law
    pumps the espresso machine
like a lady engineer
    in the cab of a steam locomotive
in Italy, after the Revolution.

I sit at my favorite table.

September 9, 1976,
    someone else's paper told me
Mao Tse-tung had died,
    ten minutes into that day.
I sat at this same corner table,
    looking at newsprint photos,
        and watched the sky stream away –
    a wooden flagpole,
a Gothic rooftop wobbly in the old glass.


*Five Photographs of Mao Tse-tung:*


*1. With Chu Teh in Yenan, 1937*

Mao scowls, a cigarette between his light fingers,
as if he has just inhaled
    and is holding his breath –
no rank on his uniform,
    his feet in cloth slippers.
Chu Teh, his best general, straddles the pavement,
    a broken brick by his sneaker.
Happiness spreads from his peasant eyes.
Mao Tse-tung,
        squinting, high-cheeked, cautious,
seems to be analysing a problem.

*2. Mao Tse-tung with bodyguards,*
   *during flight from Yenan, 1948*


A character from Chinese opera
 – his wife Chiang Ch'ing, 'Green River',
       behind him on a shaggy pony –
inconvenienced, merely
       disdainful of enemy bombers,
   their caravan small in the vast landscape.


Tribesmen in the line of march,
   dark Mongolian bodyguards –
tightness of fear in their faces.


*3. Mao Tse-tung in triumph in Peking,*
         *October, 1949*


Standing up
in a new jeep with good tyres,
wearing a black, fur-collared, new-looking coat –
   his face turned toward interminable rows
       of motorized artillery,
   freshly painted barrels raised in salute –
Mao's eyes unfocussed into the distance.


*4. Peking, undated*


A human face covering the side of a building,
Mao Tse-tung not so big as the ear
   of his portrait,
silk-suited, surrounded by diplomats and generals,

stiffly at attention on a balcony
over the head of his massive image.

Two million people
  in the Place of Heavenly Peace,
holding two million pictures of that face –
as though to answer
the ghosts of all those Mao called
    *gentry    landowners*
      *bourgeois elements,*
blood in the river of the Revolution:
*How can one say*
  *that the peasants should not now*
*rise, and shoot one or two of them*
  *and bring about*
*a small-scale reign of terror?*

*A revolution is not*
*like inviting people to dinner*
    *or writing an essay,*
        *or doing fancy needlework . . . .*

I remember the XIVth Dalai Lama
  of what is now
'The Autonomous Cultural Region of Tibet' –
in Delhi in the 60s, in exile.
He steps into a taxi
  in monk's robes, with shaved head.
The swarthy, tribal-looking bodyguards
    break off their card game
        and follow him.

'Place on one side',
   he says to his visitors,
'the dogs of this neighborhood –
and on the other side, my life.
The lives of the dogs are worth more.'
But that day in '76
      I speak of –
everything seemed to rise on one side of life,
   and recede on the other.
I was thirty-five years old.
I ordered a double espresso.
The dust-mottled bust of Dante, now gone,
   glared at me across the bar –
untiring, unresting,
   with his hook nose and predator's eyes.


A newspaper clipping,
*San Francisco Chronicle*, 'The Voice of the West':
*'Chinese Radical's Great Leap to Bay Area'.*


*The former Red Guard*
*stowed away on a boat to Hong Kong ...*
*His plaid sofa     his RCA colour TV,*
*his view of San Francisco Bay ....*
*An articulate young man,*
*he has applied to three law schools,*
*including Harvard ....*
*He has just sold a $160,000 building.*


*A certain drive, a certain*
   *assertiveness ...*
*as though the Revolution*

*equipped him with the tools*
to *make it*
    *in America.*

The rainbow trout in my daydream
    flashes in glassy water,
snags the wet fly in mid-riffle,
    fights me like a small country.
I play him quiet
    into my quiet hand underwater,
hold him in the current,
    and slip the hook out
        of his hard jaw.

The trout hangs in the current
    as if slow to feel freedom come back
        into his muscles,
    then thrashes free downstream.

Aphorisms of Ancient Sun Tzu,
        5th century BC:

*Be as swift as the wind, as secret as the forest,*
*as consuming as fire, as silent as the mountains,*
*as impenetrable as darkness, as sudden*
*as thunderbolts.*

*War is nothing but lies.*

*In throwing in troops, drop them*
*like a millstone on an egg,*
*the solid on the void.*

Mr. Giotta turns the café lights on.
It's easy to see
        the dawn now
    as Chu Teh saw it
when the Long March began:
    *Over stones and peaks worn*
*to slippery smoothness*
    *by no one knows how many*
*eons of fierce wind, rains, and snow,*
*the column of gaunt and ragged*
        *men and women,*
*fleeing Chingkanshan,*
    *began to creep single-file*
*along the jagged crest of the*
        *mountain spur ...*
*By nightfall reached a small*
*sloping ridge of solid volcanic rock*
    *where we stopped and ate*
        *half the cold rice we had brought,*
    *huddling together and linking arms,*
*passed the night*
    *shivering and coughing.*

With daybreak they crept like fog
    down an overgrown trail
over the first village:
to drop like a millstone on the enemy garrison –
    'the solid on the void'.

    *Thousands of rifles and machine-guns*
*lay buried on the long trail south ...*
    *much ammunition, much machinery,*
        *much silver.*

73

From a poem by Mao:
*I remember how vivid they were*
*as they gazed upon rivers and mountains:*
*The Chinese earth gave strength to their words –*
*and the ancient feudal lords*
*were something they scraped off their boots.*


I look around the café at faces,
    knowing so many.
Ferlinghetti comes in after work,
smiles and frowns at the same time
    as if to say:
 'Where did we meet?'
A student drinks hot chocolate and reads *Dubliners*.


In 1969
we fought all day and ran,
    and watched ourselves on network news at night.
The Revolution seemed no farther away
    than squadcar blue-lights whipping
        hypnotically through fuchsias
            in the Berkeley hills –
    fear and love in a crowd,
        a nose full of teargas,
plate glass heavily smashing.


People say '*Our* Revolution
    had its effect'.
I yawn, and nod in agreement.
But what I see is
'urban guerillas' cleaning houses,
        pumping gas,

cooking eggs at six in the morning
    for someone else,
collecting food stamps,
teaching grammar to convicts,
– revolutionized into poverty –
or invisible in some good job.
'The best minds of *my* generation' too,
        self-exiled from America,
            strangers to power,
        a wasted generation.
My teacher from college writes ' Alienation
        hovers over your lines
    like the smell of burning flesh
        over the funeral pyres'.

I put a dime in the Trieste's jukebox,
    with its unique selection
of Italian arias    Greek *bouzouki* music
    songs in Portuguese from *Black Orpheus*
    thin-air music from the high Andes
        (bass drum and flute).

Maria Callas sings
        'Un Bel Dì Vedremo.'
        Silence sinks into the café.

Remember:
*The Chinese earth gave strength to their words.*

A last photograph:

*5. Mao Tse-tung swimming the Yangtse River, 1966*

His solemn, chunky head visible
  above water
like the head of an old bull –
showing his enemies himself alive,
Mao floats on his back
  or side-strokes lazily
    crossing the two-mile river
  gazing at the changing sky –
oil refineries on the bank,
  mountains in the far distance:
*I've just drunk the waters of Changsha,*
*now I taste fish in the surf at Wuchang.*
*Let the wind blow, let rain drench me.*
*I'd rather be here*
*than wasting time in rooms of power.*
*Today I am free!*
*Old Confucius stands on the bank,*
                *observing:*
*'All nature is flowing away'.*


New cars slip through Saturday night –
headlights, red tail-lights streaking,
      rain blowing off the ocean.
I walk through North Beach
    beside and beneath neon bodies
        of unreal women.

I light an illegal cigarette
       and smoke it unnoticed through Chinatown,
over hosed-down sidewalks smelling of fish,
past the hot windows of Chinese sweatshops
       open to the night –
live pheasants in cages on the roof of a car,
       heads of cattle in buckets,
leopard sharks in shop-windows on beds of ice.

Mah-jong tiles click in below-street parlours.
   Blue light seeps through closed blinds;
red-and-white uniforms swim over TV grass.

Business picks up again at the Golden Dragon,
where blood of seventeen people
   was washed off the floor last year
and the place remodeled.

I gravitate toward my parking place,
   stepping into the baroque church
      of Our Lady of Guadalupe
to shake two junkies who are following me.

In the fragrant semi-darkness
   I touch cool water to my forehead.
The priest hands me pamphlets
   and asks God to bless me.
He stops me as I leave the church.
'God bless you', he says the second time.
       'Pray for us all.'
I promise to do that, and step outside.
       The two men are gone.

I find the car and drive out past
solid, stone-built Pacific Avenue mansions –
past bars for every kind of drinker –
past everybody and everything there is
        to buy –
past a Chinese lady in silk
    looking into the vanished sunset –
past the exquisite
three-hundred-year-old military base –
    white markers, thousands
in a forest of mist and cypresses –
out over the Golden Gate
and the spirits of all the dead.
I nudge my car into the northbound stream, alone,
    straight down the middle of the bridge,
into the redwoods and foothills,
into the open darkness.

# Easter Week: Vermont

*for Robert Fitzgerald*

Snowbanks, exhausted, melt onto pavement.
Slick stripes on the road, buttercup yellow –
A pickup truck that colour, and a sign,
Diamond-shaped, 'Frost Heaves', stuck in grey snow.

In graveyards, around tombstones, snow scooped, cupped,
Around named, sun-thawed granite and marble.
The trees, from within, push back the snowdrifts.
Maybe in wild trout today the blood moves.

Maples, five feet through, drain into buckets.
A white-haired man, his black-and-red-checked back
To me, lumbers through timber with buckets full.
Steam spouts out the tops of sugar-houses.

New birch saplings by the roadside stare
With a coldness from inside the bark
That goes back a hundred million winters.
Their nerve has survived another freeze.

The bare ground, snow-covered since November,
Turns up filter-tips, newspapers bleached of print,
Blue plastic-coated wires, styrofoam cups,
A red something, a Christmas ornament.

Flinching, cowlicked, stunned by the six-months' winter,
The grass flushes tawny, deep amethyst,
And keeps its eyes shut to the light.
An alder's leafless crown colours redly.

The landscape, in that old and simple way
Of saying just what happens, 'awakens'.
It renews itself like the unfolding
Fine linen of stored words heard once a year:

Mary Magdalene and the other Mary
At daybreak on the first day of the week
Came unto that fresh-cut word the sepulchre.
The stone, the vowels sing, was rolled away.

Two men stand by them in shining garments.
*He is not here*, they say. *He is risen.*
*Why seek ye the living among the dead?*
Tough-stemmed crocuses stir underfoot.

# from *Sewanee in Ruins*: Part I

*for Andrew Lytle*

*Ecce quam bonum et quam iucundum*
*habitare fratres in unum.*

— Psalm 133

*... bare ruin'd quires ...*

— Shakespeare

The Romantics were right.
Gothic buildings are best seen in ruins:
sky-sprung clerestories in wild brambles,
Romanesque arches reconstructed by the mind,
tumbled-over stones to stumble on in a field
of grey violets,
in a place you can no longer drive to.

When I walk by the Neo-Gothic
duPont Library at the University of the South,
its new stone rouged-up, peachy
after October rain,
my mind sees the facade stripped of half its masonry
by Virginia creeper and torn fog.
I smile into leaves of the bramble stock,
strong and ugly,
aggressively shiny in the mist.

But I come from the cemetery,
where the past is buried under stone.
I smile into the broad, pleasant faces of my students,
the black among the white

– for we are one people –;
yet my thoughts are with men I have heard of and read of
who, possessed by a fatal romanticism,
killed at fourteen,
ate corn burned in the field,
and wore the dead enemies' shoes
in 1865, when everything burned
but the brick chimneys
and a way of talking.

I touch with my tongue my four gold teeth,
answer to the name *Sir*,
and feel out of place
in my twenty-year-old tweeds
among these boys and girls
who call themselves men and women,
these ripe-peach bodies and untouched smiles,
these peacock-blue, canary-yellow, billiard-table-green
clothes from the catalogue of L.L.Bean –
initials emblazoned as on silver –
and hundreds of tiny alligators that never snap.

I climb the 1890s Gothic battlements to my classroom
and teach these fortunate young men and women
their history,
and the old lost nation's name for this spot:
Rattlesnake Springs.
Two coiled rattlesnakes spelled into a slab of rock.

*Saawaneew* in Algonquin,
though white men didn't know it,
meant The South,
from the Ohio to the Gulf of Mexico.

The words of someone's old diary or letter from 1860:
*Nine bishops in their robes*
*and 50 or 60 clergymen in surplices and gowns*
*and some 5,000 people*
*formed a procession*
*and headed by a band playing Hail Columbia*
*marched to the spot*
*where the main building of the university*
*was to be.*
*Here Old Hundred was sung by the vast multitude.*

Those confident, cotton-flush Southerners,
fifty years from the wilderness,
with their horse races, cockfights, African slaves,
their *code of duello and decanter*,
their railroad cars full of Sir Walter Scott romances,
their 19th-century optimism
and half a million cotton dollars as endowment,
founded their *'Southern Oxford'*,
*as they always called it.*

*The hogsheads of hams, the barrels, and boxes, and bags*
*of groceries, the carloads of crockery and glass, the*
*bales of sheeting and blankets, and acres of straw beds,*
*indicated that Southern hospitality for once*
*had entered upon the difficult undertaking*
*of outdoing itself ...*

*Yet even then,*
*there was a feeling as of a great danger*
*near at hand,*
*a yawning chasm which all feared to look upon ....*

83

Next April
the bells of St. Philip's and St. Michael's,
the old Charleston churches,
change-rang in celebration.
But a clearheaded observer, if one could be found,
looking off the Battery past Fort Sumter
into the immense ocean and sky,
must have felt mostly dread.

*The rest of the oft-told tale is too well known,*
*how war devastated the land*
*the two armies passed over, fighting as they went.*
*The frame houses*
*built for Bishops Elliott and Polk*
*have been burnt to the ground,*
*the cornerstone blasted to pieces by Federal troops –*
the six-ton block of marble
that 34 yoke of oxen
had dragged up the mountain from Elk River.

*We are encamped* (21st Indiana Infantry)
*on the top of the Cumberland Mountains,*
*on the site of the grand Southern University*
*that was to have been ...*
*Near our quarters is a very large spring*
*of the clearest and finest water I ever drank.*
*We expect no real fight between here and Atlanta.*

My pleasant-faced freshmen
from South Carolina, Texas, Kentucky, Alabama
laugh at the word *Yankee,*
considering my use of it a kind of local colour.
To them the great War of the Sixties
is like some football game we lost.

And I have no quarrel with them.

To wear expensive clothes,
to enjoy wearing them
– or just not to think about it –,
to go through the seasons as from one party to the next,
to know no enemies,
to turn from boy or girl May- or June-like
into man or woman,
to make 18-year-old love in the back seat of a Cadillac
on a warm Delta night –
this is the way to be young!

Not to ride and kill with Forrest all across Tennessee
or die with Jackson at Chancellorsville
or Polk at Pine Mount,
or come back from war
with health and nerves and worldly goods destroyed.

The privilege of being young,
the luxury of ignoring history –
this is what their great-great-grandfathers fought for,
though they lost.

For the flaw in their Neoclassical structure –
the evil of owning human beings –,
they paid, all of them and all of us,
punished by a vengeance only New England could devise –
though only three Tennesseans out of a hundred in 1860
had owned a slave.

The Armies of Emancipation,
having *loosed the fateful lightning*
*of His terrible swift sword,*
would be free to go West and kill Indians.
The machines tooled in that war economy
eased the North on plush velvet and iron rails
into its Gilded Age,
and reconstructed the South
with sharecropping and hunger –
and a deeper thirst,
not satisfied by the Coke you drink
flying Delta over kudzu fields out of Atlanta,
reading *The Last Gentleman* by Walker Percy.

History stopped in 1865,
then started again as memory:
the grey and gold of the good-smelling, broadcloth uniform,
the new, beautiful, handsewn battle-flag,
the West Point strategists, the Ciceronian orations,
the cavalry charges –
soldiers on a road sing 'Away, Away' –;
then the heads shot off friends' shoulders,
the desertions, the belly-killing stench of dead flesh,
the forced marches over hardscrabble Virginia roads –
and Richmond like a brick graveyard.

# Envoi

Go little book, *par avion*.
Wing, verses, toward your targets:
Where faces cool and harden behind bars,
Where an idea straps on a pistol,

Where the people eat their right to vote,
Where machine guns and TV cameras
Look from the tops of glass buildings.
Go, little peregrine.

Fly as I taught you
With bombs tucked under your wings,
In a V of attack, low to the ground,
Underneath the enemy's lazy radar ....

It's too much though – isn't it little friend?
You glide over cool marble floors
Out into the womanly moonlight.
A rosevine encircles you, you bleed on the thorns.

Your throat opens to a harmony of seasons.
You sing of the nest, of unruffled June mornings,
Of leaving the nest, of building it again;
Of its perfect circle.

*You would have me kill, you whose life is a breath?*
*I pity you, yes I pity you,* you warble,
And take off into the distance
As if you thought you would live forever.

I stand in the predawn field, boots drenched,
The big glove covering my wrist and hand,
And watch you soar, a spec now,
Into the rainy future.